contentment

content-
ment

*a godly woman's
adornment*

LYDIA BROWNBACK

CROSSWAY BOOKS
WHEATON, ILLINOIS

Contentment

Copyright © 2008 by Lydia Brownback

Published by Crossway Books
   a publishing ministry of Good News Publishers
   1300 Crescent Street
   Wheaton, Illinois 60187

Cover design: Jon McGrath

Cover illustration: iStock

First printing, 2008

Printed in the United States of America

Library of Congress Cataloging-in-Publication Data

Brownback, Lydia, 1963–
 Contentment : a godly woman's adornment / Lydia Brownback.
  p. cm. — (On-the-go devotionals ; #2)
 Includes bibliographical references.
 ISBN 978-1-58134-958-0 (tpb)
 1. Christian women—Religious life. 2. Contentment—Religious aspects—Christianity. I. Title. II. Series.
BV4527.B765   2008
248.8'43—dc22   2007044603

VP			17	16	15	14	13	12	11	10	09	08
14	13	12	11	10	9	8	7	6	5	4	3	2	1

With gratitude to God
for a season like no other:
Renee Blackburn
Tom Blackburn
Mark Brown
Tim Humeniuk
Karen Montgomery
Lore Ritscher
Susan Russack
Steve Schmidt
James Stoudt

Contents

Introduction

*Y*ou can have it all, so don't settle for less." That is what we are told. So we spend ourselves on life, liberty, and the pursuit of happiness. Realization of the American dream—the Western dream—lies at our fingertips. But that is largely the problem—so much of what we want remains just out of reach. We can touch it, but we cannot get our hands around it. And sometimes we do get hold of it, but we are not any happier. There is always something we still don't have. So we pour our lives into acquiring that one next thing. "Then I'll be happy," we say. But we are always saying that, because there is always just one more thing.

Our unhappiness does not spring from what we lack. It springs from our *desire* for what we lack. We crave love, beauty, and comfort. We crave independence and peaceful surroundings. We crave self-esteem. We crave the smooth rhythm of a balanced life—a little of this, a bit of that, but not too much of either. We are unhappy because we have come to expect such things, living as we do in a society that advocates personal rights, autonomy, and prosperity above all else.

We refuse to accept that our prosperity isn't going to make us happy, and for all of our rights, autonomy is just an illusion. Consider how we react when a storm comes and the electricity goes out. We cannot curl our hair or microwave our Lean Cuisines or click through the channels of DIRECTV. How happy are we then? But people in underdeveloped countries—those without rights or prosperity—are not unhappy when the power goes out, largely because they have spent much of their lives functioning with no electricity at all. They don't fret about limp hair. They don't sit around bored for lack of Lifetime TV. And they enjoy the little food they have with no hang-ups about high fructose levels and excessive carbohydrates.

But just as prosperity does not lock in happiness, awful circumstances don't have to lock it out. Do we believe that? Most of us don't when we are faced with unwanted singleness, an unhappy marriage, infertility, financial hardship, broken relationships, terminal illness, or regret. In such circumstances we can't imagine anything but unhappiness. What choice do we have? We do have a choice, actually. We can be happy, not necessarily in the American way, but in the biblical way. It is all a matter of what we live for. If we live for the good times, even those given to us by God, we will never find happiness because seasons of wilderness, waiting, and withholding are just as much, if not more, a part of life on this earth as seasons of ease and peace.

Happiness, or contentment, comes from where we look and what we believe, not from what we have. In determining how to think and feel about our lives, we tend to create separate categories for happiness and contentment. In our mental hierarchy we put happiness at the top. Happiness, to our way of thinking, is the pinnacle. Happiness is when we get the things we have dreamed of and when life goes our way. Contentment, so we think, is secondary. We see it as the consolation emotion we must settle for when actual happiness is lacking. "I'm not really happy with the way things are, but I'm content for now." Yet contentment and happiness are one and the same if we understand these words from a biblical perspective and orient our lives there.

That is what we will do as we work through God's Word together. As we look at what he says to us, we'll discover that he wants our contentment—our happiness—even more than we do, even in the hard times. He is not withholding it from us; we do that to ourselves. Happiness really is at our fingertips.

the
devotions

Living in the Valley

*For everything there is a season, and a time for every matter
under heaven . . . a time to break down, and a time to
build up; a time to weep, and a time to laugh;
a time to mourn, and a time to dance; . . . a time to
cast away stones, and a time to gather stones together;
a time to embrace, and a time to refrain from embracing;
a time to seek, and a time to lose; . . . a time to love,
and a time to hate; a time for war, and a time for peace.*

ECCLESIASTES 3:1-8

*L*aughter and tears, love and loss, work and play—such
words sum up the rhythm of life. Most of us will pass through
each of these seasons at one point or another, perhaps repeat-
edly, because they are God's ordering for the human race in
every age and time. But as we pass through some of these purposes, we do not feel much like singing about it as the Byrds
did in 1965. We fight against the weeping, the mourning, the
casting away, and the losing while striving to keep our lives
entrenched in the laughter, the dancing, the embracing, and
the peace.

The fight is quite natural, of course. We all prefer the
mountaintops to the valleys. But the God who has ordered

life to flow in and out of such seasons is the same God who has provided for our contentment in *every* season. Contentment is possible not only on the mountaintops but in the valleys as well. How can we mourn or lose or weep with contentment? That seems totally contradictory. And indeed we cannot if our contentment hinges on getting out of the valley, because we have no control over the beginning or ending of the seasons that God appoints for each of us.

[Contentment in the valleys comes when we stop fighting so hard to climb out. God is the one who leads us into the valleys, and he will lead us back out in his time. God ordains valleys for our good; why else would a good and kind God allow them? Trusting God in our hard times is the way to contentment—not just trusting him to get us out, but trusting his goodness while we are still in them.]If we will not trust him in the bad times, we are not going to trust him in the good times either. A friend of mine enjoyed a financially prosperous season a few years back, and she bought a beautiful home. Yet she wasn't able to enjoy it, she said, because "life is so good right now, but I know it can't last. I'm always waiting for the axe to fall."

Do we live like that, fighting so hard to stay on the peaks and to avoid the valleys? If so, we will never be happy in either place. However, if we will trust God in whichever place we find ourselves, we will know contentment whether the season is easy or hard. We will find peace in the hard times because a good Father is controlling them, and we will not be anxious in the good times because our happiness is not bound up in having to maintain them. Good times are designed to come and go, but contentment is designed to be constant for all who are in Christ.

Could It Be Sin?

Joshua said, "Alas, O Lord GOD, why have you brought this people over the Jordan at all, to give us into the hands of the Amorites, to destroy us? Would that we had been content to dwell beyond the Jordan!"

JOSHUA 7:7

*J*oshua knew better, of course. He knew that God had brought the Israelites into the Promised Land to bless them, not to destroy them. But he was frustrated because they had just lost what should have been an easy-to-win battle against the Amorites. What was God doing?

We find ourselves in similar situations from time to time, and when we do, we, too, are baffled about what God is up to. We are careful to follow God's ways, and we believe his promises, and yet our circumstances are just not working out. In the midst of his discouragement, Joshua wished he had never taken his preceding steps of risky faith. How much easier life was before! In the moment he forgets that life beyond the Jordan had been nothing but wilderness; his trust in God's faithfulness and his joy in the Promised Land are obliterated by one defeat.

Our contentment evaporates just as quickly when things go wrong in our lives. We begin to think back on an easier time, a time that, while perhaps not perfect, held a lot less pressure.

For Joshua, the Promised Land was surely much nicer than the wilderness, but at least in the wilderness someone else—Moses—had been in charge. Now Joshua was leading the Israelites, and the weight of the Amorite defeat fell squarely on his shoulders. But God had a reason for the defeat, and rather than allowing Joshua to wallow in misery, he answered his cry. "Get up!" the Lord said. "Why have you fallen on your face? Israel has sinned. . . . There are devoted things in your midst, O Israel. You cannot stand before your enemies until you take away the devoted things from among you" (Josh. 7:10, 13). Unbeknownst to Joshua, an Israelite named Achan had failed to follow God's express orders to destroy all the treasures, the "devoted things," taken from their enemies in battle. Achan kept back a little of these riches for himself, and his secretive act was what had brought great trouble on the entire Israelite army.

Could our present trial be the result of sin? If so, we won't have to look far to find it. We don't have to engage in endless speculation about what our sin might be; God is always willing to show us our sin. Sometimes, though, we refuse to see it, or we minimize it. "Well, I am still struggling to give up that bad habit, but it's such a little thing. How could that have anything to do with my difficulty?" But God does not ask us to connect all the dots. He just asks us to be obedient. If there is a connection, God will make it, just like he did with Joshua. Maybe there is a connection between our unrepentant sin and our difficulty, and maybe not. The point isn't to figure out if there is a connection and then to obey—it is simply to obey. We cannot rightly ask for or expect to be restored to a place of peace and to see God's blessings on our lives if we are treating sin lightly.

Are you finding your circumstances frustrating right now? If so, God has a good reason. Perhaps it is his way of getting you to deal with your sin. Rather than turning back to an easier time in your life, turn to God and examine your heart. He will gladly show you sin that you may be harboring. He showed Joshua, and Joshua purged out the wrong with no delay. Afterward victory against the Amorites came easily.

Today, Not Tomorrow or Yesterday

Now the rabble that was among them had a strong craving.
And the people of Israel also wept again and said,
"Oh that we had meat to eat! We remember the fish
we ate in Egypt that cost nothing, the cucumbers,
the melons, the leeks, the onions, and the garlic.
But now our strength is dried up, and there is nothing at all
but this manna to look at."

NUMBERS 11:4-6

*S*trong cravings—we all have them. The single who longs for marriage, the wife who longs for a baby, the terminated employee who longs for new work. Many of the things we crave are good things, and therefore our desire for them is also good. But when we focus almost exclusively on our desires and unmet needs, what is good becomes bad. It becomes obsessive. It becomes a craving, and we aren't content to live without the thing we want or need.

We find ourselves baffled with God. After all, why does he even allow us to experience such intense desire only to leave us unfulfilled? Why would a good God do that? There are many reasons why God does that, all of them for our benefit. Not only does he strengthen us through the process, but he also teaches us to depend solely on him and to enjoy what he provides. He provides for the single woman by giving her friends, fellowship, and meaningful work. He provides for the childless woman by giving her opportunities to mother in other ways. And he provides, often miraculously, ways for the unemployed woman to meet her expenses. Whatever we long for but lack is an area in which God will reveal himself to be adequate for us.

Since that is true, the source of our misery is not that we lack the thing we long for; our misery comes from wanting that thing so much that we are not open to recognizing or receiving any alternative. Contentment comes as we wait on God's timetable and as we trust that what he provides in the midst of our lack is really all we need until he provides something else.

Obsessing on something we want skews our perspective not only on the present but also on the past. In the midst of their craving, the Israelites remembered the fish they had eaten in Egypt "that cost nothing" but in reality had cost them everything. They had been slaves in Egypt when they ate that fish, slaves who were horribly treated. "Maybe I should have been more open to Tom," Ginny reflected when her marriage to Ben failed to turn out as she had hoped. "After all, he had great earning potential." But Ginny is forgetting that she stopped considering Tom as a marriage partner because he was lacking in fervor for Christ. Single or married, rich or poor, focusing on what we do not have warps our memory.

Obsessing on an unmet desire also takes away our joy and delight in all that God has provided for us today. The Israelites had manna in abundance—tasty food that simply fell from the sky. Yet their enjoyment of it was completely lost. If we focus our thoughts on looking only at what we hope tomorrow will bring, we will miss all the pleasure of today. Life is made up of todays, not tomorrows. What do we have today? Whatever it may be—a good friend, a hug, a freshly baked bagel, sunshine, a place to call home—can bring us joy because it is God's gift for our enjoyment. Taking joy in the little things is contentment.

The Good Old Days

Say not, "Why were the former days better than these?"
For it is not from wisdom that you ask this.

ECCLESIASTES 7:10

"Life was so good back then. How did I end up here?"
When pressures mount, memories of the good old days rise
up in our minds more frequently. We long for a simpler time.
The problems of yesterday were so much easier to handle
than those we face today. That is the lie of nostalgia. It takes
our memories and paints them with rosy colors. We forget
that we left much of yesterday behind for good reason.

That being said, the good old days really were better
for some of us—the time before we got sick, lost our child,
our job, our spouse. We lament like Naomi who said, "The
Almighty has dealt very bitterly with me. I went away full,
and the LORD has brought me back empty" (Ruth 1:20–21).
How can we not long to recapture the time when life worked?
We would do anything to go back. But no matter how fond
the memories—real or rose-colored—we cannot go back.
Anyone who has tried knows that just doesn't work. But that
does not leave us with nothing. We do have options, which is
what the preacher was getting at in Ecclesiastes. We may not
be able to change our circumstances, but we can change the
way we think about them.

The unwise option, as the preacher points out, is to make mental comparisons between then and now. Yesterday will always have an unfair advantage because we remember selectively. Plus comparing in this way is really nothing more than mental grumbling. While remembering fondly is good, remembering with lament is not, springing, as it does, from the same outlook Naomi had—"the Almighty has dealt very bitterly with me."

We have another option, however. We can look upward instead of backward, and when we do, we will find hope. Hope always lies ahead of us, never behind. Naomi found it. Her path back began with a return to her people, the Lord's people. His blessings and provision for us during hard times will always be found among his people. It is there that we see his hand at work and his character revealed.

Sometimes we are cut off from God's people for one reason or another, but even then we are not shut off from God himself. We have his Word in front of us and his Spirit within us, and they work together to show us who God is in the midst of present difficulties.

When we look at God—among his people, in his Word, and by his Spirit—we are going to realize that the present is actually better than the past. It is better because God is the one who brought us where we are today. And the God who led us here is good, kind, and, let's not forget, purposeful. Everything he does in our lives, everywhere he leads us, is designed to fulfill his primary intention for us, which is to know him better. Contentment does not lie around the next corner. It is not waiting for us on the other side of today's difficulty, nor is it lost with yesterday. Contentment is where God is, and God is with us today.

I Can't . . . I Won't!

Now the LORD *God appointed a plant and made it
come up over Jonah, that it might be a shade over his head,
to save him from his discomfort. So Jonah was exceedingly
glad because of the plant. But when dawn came up the next
day, God appointed a worm that attacked the plant,
so that it withered. When the sun rose, God appointed
a scorching east wind, and the sun beat down on the head
of Jonah so that he was faint. And he asked that he might die
and said, "It is better for me to die than to live."
But God said to Jonah, "Do you do well to be angry
for the plant?" And he said, "Yes, I do well to be angry,
angry enough to die."*

JONAH 4:6–9

Kara doesn't anticipate the end of the workday any more than Jonah wanted to come out from under the plant. A few minutes before 5 each day, Kara's colleagues are already shutting down their PCs and packing up, eager to get home or wherever it is they are going. But Kara has no one to go home to, and come the end of a long day, she is usually too tired to call friends to go out. Long after her colleagues have left the office, Kara heads toward her empty condo where she

makes herself something to eat and settles down in front of
the television. She rarely finds anything worth watching, but
the programs fill the empty hours until bedtime.

Recently, however, her evening routine has been troubling
her conscience. Much of what she sees on television is in
violation of Paul's words: "Whatever is true . . . honorable
. . . commendable . . . think about these things" (Phil. 4:8).
So for a few evenings Kara turns off the television, gets hold
of some good books, and sits down to read instead. But the
overwhelming silence intensifies her loneliness. "I just can't
do this!" she cries, and the very next night she is back on the
couch with the clicker.

That scenario has played out in Kara's life many times this
year. She has made several attempts to heed the Spirit-given
weight on her conscience, but each time the silence pressed in,
and she gave up in frustration. Eventually the nagging sense
of wrong just went away. Something else went away too,
however—now Kara feels distant from God, and it is becoming more and more difficult to recognize him as a friend in the
midst of her loneliness.

The Holy Spirit comes in this way to all of us at times,
placing his finger on something in our lives that he insists
must change. But when the thing he pinpoints touches on an
extremely sensitive area, we say, "Lord, you can't possibly
ask me to deal with this now! Maybe later when things are
better . . ." But saying no to God is foolish, not only because
God has a right to our immediate obedience, but also because
God is the only real remedy for our unhappiness, and he
knows that the things to which we cling for comfort are actually robbing us of blessing. We cut ourselves off from our one

source of help and choose instead to stay comfortable in our pitiable, self-made remedies.

Underlying Kara's resistance to change is resentment, although she does not see this clearly. She is mad at God because she is lonely, and she thinks God is unfair to ask her to give up her electronic consolation. Kara feels entitled to her evening activity because she believes God has deprived her of companionship. But her thinking is all backward. Her evening activity is actually enhancing the very thing from which she longs to be free—her loneliness.

God always works to free us from the tactics we use to avoid dealing with hard things, because he knows that our tactics are ineffective. Stepping out in obedience, even when we can't understand why or where it will lead, is the only way we will find the peace we are yearning for and help for our hurts.

My Share

Someone in the crowd said to him, "Teacher,
tell my brother to divide the inheritance with me."

LUKE 12:13

"The larger the estate, the greater the rift." How true this often is, and how sad. Rather than bonding together over the shared loss of a parent, siblings destroy their familial relationships, fighting over who gets the mahogany table, the hand-painted china, and the costly string of pearls. Even more regrettable is the fact that such squabbles are common in Christian families.

"We got the blue dishes, but everyone knows the red ones are better."

"She got the clock and that set of crystal, while I got only that old painting."

"I'm not asking for everything; I just want my share."

In some cases, maybe in yours, the goods were not divided equally, and you ended up with less than your sister. Or maybe you received a smaller pay increase than your undeserving coworker, or after months of hard work an honorable committee position was given to a newcomer instead of to you. In such cases we can certainly do what the man in the crowd did. He asked Jesus for help. "Teacher, tell my brother to divide the inheritance with me."

We can pray, "Lord, work in my sister's heart so that she sees how unfair this is," but the answer we will get is the same answer that Jesus gave to this man: "Man, who made me a judge or arbitrator over you?" (Luke 12:14). And he turned to all who were listening and said to them, "Take care, and be on your guard against all covetousness, for one's life does not consist in the abundance of his possessions" (v. 15).

The first thing Jesus did was to clear up misconceptions about who he is (v. 14). He did that then, and he does it today. We will never know contentment in Christ if we seek him as a divine referee, however unfairly we may have been treated. His work in our lives is not about making sure we get the maximum benefits in the here and now, even when we are entitled to those benefits. In fact, real contentment often comes when we willingly embrace the loss of them.

The second thing Jesus does is reveal the spirit of covetousness that underlies most of our prayers about obtaining our share. Fighting over things is something we are to guard against because all such fighting is sin. But Jesus does more than simply place his finger on the sin problem; he provides a remedy for it by redirecting our thinking to the place of peace. We will never find contentment—freedom from that angry feeling of unfairness—by getting the things that are rightfully ours. We will find it by letting go of our entitlement to them.

At Any Cost?

*Now Naboth the Jezreelite had a vineyard in Jezreel,
beside the palace of Ahab king of Samaria.
And after this Ahab said to Naboth,
"Give me your vineyard, that I may have it for a
vegetable garden, because it is near my house, and I will
give you a better vineyard for it; or, if it seems good to you,
I will give you its value in money." But Naboth said
to Ahab, "The LORD forbid that I should give you the
inheritance of my fathers." And Ahab went into his house
vexed and sullen because of what Naboth the Jezreelite
had said to him, for he had said, "I will not give you
the inheritance of my fathers." And he lay down on his bed
and turned away his face and would eat no food.*

1 KINGS 21:1–4

*P*ower, prestige, and paychecks—enough of all three
undoubtedly makes life easier in some ways. But each has its
pitfalls too. Because Ahab was king of Israel, he had more
than anyone in the nation. Yet for all his wealth he couldn't
get everything he wanted. He wanted his neighbor's back-

yard, and when his request was denied he fell into a funk. But his not having that land wasn't the real cause of his self-pity. It was the fact that someone stood in his way.

One of the reasons we pour ourselves into acquiring more money, power, and prestige is so we can get what we want and avoid what we hate.

"The neighborhood is changing, and not for the better. Let's move uptown."

"I know you don't like to spend money eating out, but I do. If you come with me, I'll pick up the check."

"She has no right to talk to me like that! I've been serving on this committee a lot longer than she has!"

Because he was king, Ahab could have taken Naboth's land by force. But Ahab didn't pull rank on Naboth. In fact, he made him a generous offer for the vineyard. But his attempt at generosity was nothing more than a shiny veneer covering his demanding, self-seeking heart. Are we like Ahab? We are if we find ourselves frustrated and angry when our resources of time, effort, money, and verbal finesse fail to solve a problem or to bring about something we hope for. We are if, like Ahab, we allow the lack of one thing to ruin our enjoyment of all else we have—the single woman who wants a husband so badly that she cannot appreciate her friends, her job, her home, or her church; the wife who stops building into her marriage because pregnancy just isn't happening; the gifted Bible teacher who won't use her skills at all because she is told she cannot use them from the pulpit.

What are we to do when all our efforts fail and we can't get something we want? We can demand it at any cost, which is what Ahab did. In the long run he got the vineyard, but only because he joined in a plot to have Naboth killed. We

can get a lot of things by sidestepping God's ways, but whatever we get in wrong ways will bring only more misery. There
is, however, a better answer: we can let go. Isn't it better to
go without if God is not the giver? Everything on earth lies at
God's beck and call, and therefore he is well able to provide
us the thing we long for if it seems good to him to do so. Are
we willing to let go and leave the matter in his hands? If we
will just let go, we will find ourselves content with or without
our heart's desire.

Cravings and Camels

But as for me, my feet had almost stumbled,
my steps had nearly slipped. For I was envious of
the arrogant when I saw the prosperity of the wicked.

P S A L M 7 3 : 2 - 3

A happy marriage, three healthy children, unlimited financial resources, a large and beautifully appointed home with hired help to clean it—most women's idea of the perfect life. Mallory, someone I know, lives that life. She has ample money and time to develop her skills at various hobbies and to exercise her creative talent in decorating her home. She delights in entertaining, whether her friends or her husband's business associates, and she devotes much energy into creating fun-filled activities for her children. Mallory is the pin that pricks my envy. *Doesn't she realize how good she has it?* I think when she describes her latest stress about her house, her hobbies, or her teenaged daughters.

Unbeknownst to Mallory, God has used her mightily in my life. In the few short months I've known her, I have come to see that Mallory doesn't have it all. In fact, she really has very little because she doesn't know the Lord. For all her family and material blessing, she is lost inside, which is why finding the perfect prom dress for her daughter is for her a very real problem. Her confidence lies solely in how well she can manage her material world and hold her family together. She can't, of course, which is why, dream-come-true life and all, Mallory isn't happy. I do not have the home or the abundance of material blessings that Mallory does, but I know the Lord. He is mine, and I am his. In reality, therefore, I have it all, and Mallory has little.

Asaph, who wrote Psalm 73, was envious because those who don't follow God seem to have an easier time of it. And in many ways, initially at least, that is true. But from an eternal perspective, having a lot isn't necessarily a blessing. The more we have, the more self-sufficient we deceive ourselves into thinking we are. The rich of this world may have material comforts, but if God is far from their minds and hearts, they really have nothing.

Christians often lack the things the world has because the lack forces us to turn to God and to depend on his provision. Lack, therefore, facilitates closeness to God in a way that prosperity rarely does. Jesus is the one who said, "Only with difficulty will a rich person enter the kingdom of heaven. Again I tell you, it is easier for a camel to go through the eye of a needle than for a rich person to enter the kingdom of God" (Matt. 19:23–24).

"He who did not spare his own Son but gave him up for us all, how will he not also with him graciously give us all things?" (Rom. 8:32). Can we not be content if part of the "all things" includes some withholding? For the daughter of God, any withholding is itself a provision, and we can experience it with joy when we know that the withholder loves us.

Contentment Is a Choice

Keep your life free from love of money, and be content
with what you have, for he has said,
"I will never leave you nor forsake you."

*A*re you content with what you have—with your calling in life, your marital status, your income bracket, your
home? Most of us must admit there are times and seasons
when we really struggle to accept how God has ordered
our lives. A little shift here, and a bit of tweaking there, we
think, and we'd be content. So we strive at the tweaking,
but in the process we find that new things to adjust keep
cropping up. So forward we go, pouring our energy into
changing what we can because we believe happiness lies in
settling things just so. But contentment won't be found in
changing the things we don't like about our lives, which is
what the author of Hebrews is telling us.

In his words we find why contentment is possible, even
when we lack our heart's desires. We can be content with our
lives exactly as they are today because God has promised he is
always with us. Our problem really isn't that we need something we don't have; our problem is that we don't find God
to be enough for us. Many of us can't even comprehend how

God can meet us in our empty places and satisfy us fully. We are open to the idea, but we just don't see how it's possible.

Sometimes we get a wrong idea about how God satisfies us. He doesn't come to us on our terms, taking the role of a surrogate for the things or the relationships we lack. He comes in place of those things, giving us something even better. The whole reason we can't resonate with the words of Hebrews 13:5 is that we are bound up in the things of this life and our desires for them. If we would just look away from those, we would find that God delights to fill up our empty places with joy, peace, guidance, love, security, and communion with him through his Spirit. Once we get a taste of that, we find that it is no second-best consolation prize. We will find it to be better, richer, fuller than any earthly relationship or material blessing.

We can find this for ourselves by guarding against focusing overly much on what this world offers. We can—and should—certainly enjoy the material things God gives us, but only if we hold them loosely. It is the love of this world's blessings, the focus on getting them, that is the problem, not the blessings themselves.

We don't need anything more than what we have right now, today, in order to be content. The Bible says so; therefore it must be true. The choice is ours.

There's No Place Like Home

By faith Abraham obeyed when he was called to go out
to a place that he was to receive as an inheritance.
And he went out, not knowing where he was going.

*H*ouses can be built in a month, but it takes years to build a home. That's because home is much more than the place in which we live. Home is people and routine and familiarity and refuge. Home is where we fit; it's a sense of belonging. Home is the God-ordained anchor for the rhythm of earthly life. The deeper the roots of home, the more of our identity is wrapped up in it. Sooner or later, though, we are called to leave home, and it is often not until then that we discover just how deeply our souls are entrenched. Teenagers head off to college, professionals face job transfers, and missionaries are sent overseas. And no matter how good and right and exciting the opportunity, there is a sadness.

What we call *home* is always changing. Sometimes it is not we who leave home; it is home that leaves us. It changed for me when my brother got engaged to be married. I was thrilled with the prospect of a sister-in-law, and I loved the woman he'd chosen, but mixed into my joy was a good bit of sadness. My brother was, in a very real sense, leaving our family to start a new one of his own. "Every change, no matter how good, involves loss," my mother told me at the time, and over the years I've learned how very right she was.

When we are the ones who leave, we find that the excitement of our new adventure fades quickly, and once it does, homesickness so easily creeps in. We miss our family. We miss our friends. We miss our church. We miss the familiarity. We miss the unconditional acceptance. There's isolation in the pressure we feel to hide who we really are until we know people well enough to let our guard down. There's strangeness in having to rely on MapQuest to get, well, everywhere. For those who leave home often, starting over yet again— new friends, new church, new neighborhood—feels like a heavy weight.

Leaving a well-established home was one of the most difficult things I ever experienced. The homesickness was overwhelming. Where did I belong? Where was I going— really? To whom did I belong? Did my presence or absence in a particular place really matter to anyone? I didn't know who I was anymore. But God was teaching me something important, not only about home but about his people, about you and me. Home is not who we are. And all we have at home is not where our comfort and security really lie. If we seek contentment from home, we will never find it because all that makes a home *home* is constantly shifting. Either we leave or someone else does. Our employer comes under new management, turning a good job sour. Our church falls apart because the pastor has a moral failure. Home is a lot more fragile than we realize.

Back then I was learning this lesson, but in the unfamiliarity of yet another new place I was still homesick. I

questioned my decision to live so far from home. Had I done
the right thing? Life was good in the new place, but I missed
my people, my church, and the customs of my community.
Right around this time I learned that a pastor friend had been
approached about pastoring a church in the town where he'd
grown up, a town far away from where he was currently
serving. Despite being far from home, my friend had made
a lifetime commitment to the church where he served, and
I wondered how he was handling what was surely a strong
temptation to return to his roots. When I asked him, he was
honest about how very appealing the offer had been to him
and his wife, but he said, "We aren't taking the offer because
this life isn't about going home."

His words uncover for all of us the path to contentment in
a faraway place. Contentment comes when we discover that
home is much more about where we are going than where we
have come from. Home is about the people of God more than
about our families on earth. But that doesn't mean we must
do without the blessings of home in the here and now. Here
is God's promise: "Father of the fatherless and protector of
widows is God in his holy habitation. God settles the solitary
in a home" (Ps. 68:5–6a).

We can have the contentment of home right now, wherever we are, because home for us is wherever God has us. In
fact, home is more than this—home is Christ, who unites us
to God our Father. In this home alone can we find contentment because it is the only home that we will never have to
leave.

The Happy Face of Hannah

Then the woman went her way and ate,
and her face was no longer sad.

1 SAMUEL 1:18B

*H*annah had a husband, Elkanah, who loved her, but she lacked something she wanted very badly—a baby. In fact, she wanted a child so badly that she was unable to enjoy her marriage and the other blessings God had given her. Fueling her misery was her husband's other wife, Peninnah. Hannah was the wife more loved, but Peninnah had the babies, and she rubbed that fact in Hannah's face every day.

Perhaps you can relate to Hannah. So many women who desire children are unable to have them for one reason or another. If you are one of them, you know that the ache can be excruciating. It might be so painful in your case that it's harming your marriage and your ability to live fruitfully in day-to-day life. You know this is happening, but you don't know what to do about it.

Hannah did not know either, nor did her husband. The intensity of Hannah's desire brought grief to Elkanah, causing him to ask, "Hannah, why do you weep? And why do you not eat? And why is your heart sad? Am I not more to you than ten sons?" (v. 8). The Bible tells us that things went on this way in Hannah's life "year by year" (v. 7). It is God who determined to include these details in his Word, and from that fact we can know assuredly that he is not immune to the pain such women feel.

Finally Hannah came to her wits' end, and she poured her heart out to God in prayer. She was honest with God, telling him of her absolute anguish and her all-consuming desire to have a child. After she prayed in this way her sorrow ceased. The Bible tells us that she "went her way and ate" (v. 18); in other words, she got up from her prayer and went on with her life. How was she able to do so? Her desire had not diminished, nor had she received the thing for which she'd prayed so earnestly, nor was she given any guarantee that God would give her the thing she most wanted. Yet Hannah was content.

Hannah found contentment the same way we can in the midst of our most powerful yet unfulfilled desires—she gave all her longing, sorrow, and crushed hopes into the hands of the God who loved her, the one who was well able to help. But when Hannah prayed, she did more than ask God for a baby; she gave him her heart. Once she did her pain ceased, because in giving God her heart, she was set free to let him decide the outcome. That's what always happens when we really turn over to God our hearts and the things that hold them.

From Hannah we learn that getting the thing we so badly want isn't really what we need to be happy. Hannah was happy long before God answered her prayer. What we need is to know God—his character and kind intentions toward us—and we can only really know him if we give ourselves unreservedly to him. When God has our hearts, we will find that we don't need the object of our desire quite as much as we did before. Something even better fills that empty place. That is the whole reason why Hannah went her way with a face that was no longer sad.

In the long run Hannah got way more than she'd asked for: "In due time Hannah conceived and bore a son, and she called his name Samuel, for she said, 'I have asked for him from the LORD'" (v. 20). She got her baby, but long before that, she received the real desire of her heart—God himself. God may work in our circumstances like he did in Hannah's, blessing us with the things we plead for. Or he may not. Just as was true in Hannah's situation, there are no guarantees. But getting out of our misery is guaranteed if only we will give our heart to God.

> *Now to him who is able to do far more abundantly than all that we ask or think, according to the power at work within us, to him be glory in the church and in Christ Jesus throughout all generations, forever and ever. Amen. (Eph. 3:20–21).*

Rachel Repeats

When Rachel saw that she bore Jacob no children,
she envied her sister. She said to Jacob,
"Give me children, or I shall die!"

GENESIS 30:1

*J*acob's wife Rachel was never a very happy person. She wasn't a very productive woman either. She spent the majority of her life seeking the things she wanted at any cost and at the expense of other people. The Bible tells us Rachel was a beautiful woman; perhaps, as sometimes happens, her beauty gave her a misplaced sense of entitlement. But whatever the motivation, her selfish pursuits brought turmoil to all around her.

Although Leah, Rachel's older sister, was entitled to be married first according to the custom of the day, the patriarch Jacob wanted to marry Rachel; however, he got tricked into marrying Leah. While this was certainly unfair to Rachel, she really had no right to the claim of primary wife in the first place. In keeping with custom, some men back then took more than one wife, which is why Jacob wound up married to both sisters. But it was Rachel's petulance that dominated the household.

Leah, the less loved sister, was the fertile one and produced sons for Jacob. Rachel envied her sister and wanted children of her own, which she demanded from her husband. "Give me children, or I shall die!" But the exasperated Jacob replied, "Am I in the place of God, who has withheld from you the fruit of the womb?" (v. 2). Jacob's angry reply didn't deter Rachel. She forced her servant into the role of surrogate, acquiring a child through the illicit union of Bilhah and her husband. But that didn't satisfy her either.

One of Leah's sons brought home some coveted mandrake plants one day, a plant known for its narcotic qualities and for aiding in conception, and Rachel demanded the mandrakes for herself, manipulating the family to get them. Rachel said to Leah, "Please give me some of your son's mandrakes." But Leah replied, "Is it a small matter that you have taken away my husband? Would you take away my son's mandrakes also?" Rachel said, "Then he may lie with you tonight in exchange for your son's mandrakes" (vv. 14–15). She always had an agenda.

Eventually Rachel did bear a child, Joseph, but rather than thanking God for the blessing, she said, "May the LORD add to me another son!" (v. 24). She stole from her father; she manipulated her sister, and she whined and complained to her husband. The narrative seems to suggest that, in Rachel's mind, everyone around her was a means to an end. Finally Rachel died while giving birth to her second son. She died as she had lived—laboring hard for that one next thing she just had to have. God never satisfied Rachel, which is precisely why nothing else satisfied her either.

We aren't as different from Rachel as we'd like to think:

"If I could just get married, I'd be happy," says a single woman.

"If I could just get pregnant, life would be complete," says a married woman.

"If we just had another child," says a mother.

"If only my kids would give me grandchildren," says an empty nester.

"If only I had a bigger house," says a condo owner.

But when we get the "if only" we want so badly, it fails to satisfy; so we set our sights and energy on getting the next thing. Rachel lived her entire life stuck in that mind-set, but we don't have to. We can avoid living as Rachel repeats. We can live for something other than what we have or want; we can live for God. When we pour our desires away from ourselves and into God and his purposes instead, we find a deep satisfaction that nothing else can give us. Ironically, we will also find that our clamor for the next thing has somehow disappeared.

It's All in Your Mind

*I appeal to you therefore, brothers, by the mercies of God,
to present your bodies as a living sacrifice, holy and
acceptable to God, which is your spiritual worship.
Do not be conformed to this world, but be transformed
by the renewal of your mind, that by testing
you may discern what is the will of God, what is good
and acceptable and perfect.*

ROMANS 12:1-2

*H*eather's thirtieth birthday is just two months away, and she is frustrated and discouraged. Her two best friends have both gotten married this year, but there are no prospects for marriage on Heather's horizon, and she aches to be married. On top of that, she feels stuck in a job for which she is ill-suited. Heather has also experienced some annoying health issues this year, nothing life-threatening but disruptive nonetheless. As each new trial hits, Heather's discouragement grows, and her heart gets harder toward God. She doesn't understand—when will blessing come? Her friends are getting husbands and great jobs—when will it be her turn? Heather's friends offer sympathy and encouragement, but the words she is hearing aren't helping her very much. Sympathy is not going to lead Heather to a place of contentment, nor will words of encouragement if they offer no more than hollow promises that things will get better.

Heather is miserable because she has a wrong view of God and the way he works in the lives of his children—a wrong view held by many of us. God does not call us to himself in order to grant all our heart's desires, to maximize all our gifts and talents, or to keep us free from physical maladies. If that is our understanding of how the Christian life works, we will never know contentment. If we hold this view, we also are going to believe that God has let us down when life doesn't work out for us. Heather thinks this way, which is why her heart grows increasingly hard toward God.

Because God loves us, he certainly blesses our lives with lots of good things. He gives us many of our heart's desires and provides for us abundantly. But because he loves us, he also withholds some blessings for reasons that are not always plain to us. So if we set our hearts on what we want God to do for us or on what we think he should do for us, dissatisfaction with life and with God is inevitable.

The primary reason God withholds certain blessings, the lack of which creates big, empty places in our hearts and lives, is so he can fill those empty places with himself. He cannot fill with the best what is already full with the mediocre. We will never experience Christ as best if we set our hearts on what we want God to do for us in the here and now. That is Heather's real problem. She wants what God will do for her more than she wants God himself. If she would just nourish a desire for God that becomes greater than her desires for his blessings, she would realize total fulfillment—as would we—because satisfaction in him is the one desire he has

guaranteed to fulfill. Jesus promised, "Blessed are those who
hunger and thirst for righteousness, for they shall be satisfied" (Matt. 5:6).

Heather's circumstances may all work out. But maybe they
won't. So if she keeps her heart set on good days ahead, she
may never find her way out of depression. The only way out
is the discovery and embracing of what the Christian life really
is—trusting in the great love our Father has for us, exploring
the inexhaustible blessings of our union with Christ, and living for his kingdom rather than for our own. How do we get
there? Can we really want that more than we want the things
of this life that grip our hearts? We can indeed, but not by
teeth-gritting effort. David Powlison writes:

> One psychologist has put it this way: "The longings of the human
> heart cannot be changed. And even if they could, to do so would
> make mankind less than God designed us to be. Our longings
> are legitimate. They should be actively felt and embraced in
> order that we may more richly know God as the Great Satisfier
> and Lover of the human soul. The problem is not centrally with
> our longings." On the contrary, the problem is with our long-
> ings; the cravings of the human heart can be changed. . . . God
> would have us long for Him instead. To make us truly human
> God must change what we want, for we must learn to want
> the things Jesus wanted. . . . The human life is a great paradox.
> Those who die to self, find self. . . . If I crave happiness, I will
> receive misery. If I crave to be loved, I will receive rejection. If
> I crave significance, I will receive futility. If I crave control, I will
> receive chaos. If I crave reputation, I will receive humiliation. But
> if I long for God and His wisdom, I will receive God and His wis-
> dom. Along the way, sooner or later, I will also receive happiness,
> love, meaning, order, and glory.[1]

---

[1]David Powlison, *Dynamics of Biblical Change* (Glenside, PA: WTS and CCEF, 1995), 49.

When the Thorns Pierce

For the sake of Christ, then, I am content with weaknesses,
insults, hardships, persecutions, and calamities.

2 Corinthians 12:10

*T*he apostle Paul had a distracting problem, a situation that hindered his life in some way about which we are not told. His thorn may have been a physical ailment. Perhaps it was a personal sorrow or regret or the loss of something or someone he loved. Whatever it was, it caused him to plead with the Lord for relief.

Most of us have a thorn or two also. For some it's a bad memory that creeps up on us in the midst of a happy day and steals our joy. For others it's a physical limitation that prevents us from living fully productive lives. Some are burdened by the thorn of poverty, lacking the funds necessary for even the bare essentials. Perhaps it's the grief of a wayward child catapulting toward destruction through repetitive bad choices. For still others it is the pain of a long-held but unmet desire. Our thorns come in all shapes and sizes—emotional, physical, material—and they can steal our ability to be content if we don't handle them as Paul handled his thorn.

The first thing Paul did when overwhelmed by his thorn was to pray for relief, something he did on more than one

occasion. The Bible tells us that he persisted in prayer, as we
do in the midst of ongoing turmoil. But Paul's thorn was not
removed. Confronted with similar circumstances, what we
often do is to sit down and analyze whether we are praying
correctly or fervently enough. We might also seek advice
from others about why God isn't answering; we really want
to know if we are doing something wrong. Simultaneously
we go on a hunt for our hidden sin issues and try to clean
up our spiritual act. *Maybe*, we think, *my faith is just too
weak*.

But Paul did none of these things. Because his relationship with God was an intimate one, he had a listening heart
that enabled him to hear and understand God's purpose in
allowing the thorn to remain. And because his whole life was
oriented around Christ, he was able to embrace what Christ
told him: "My grace is sufficient for you, for my power is
made perfect in weakness" (v. 9). That was enough for Paul,
as his response reveals. "I will boast all the more gladly of
my weaknesses," he wrote, "so that the power of Christ may
rest upon me."

God's purpose for us is no different from his purpose for
Paul. He brings thorns because they weaken us, and it is only
when we are weak that we will be able to recognize—and
desire—the sort of strength that we can find only in Christ.
Thorns break us of our self-sufficiency. Christ's power is
made perfect, or complete, in the void created by our pow-
erlessness to help ourselves out of a painful place. Because
of his thorn, Paul learned the benefit of this great exchange,
which enabled him to write, "When I am weak, then I am
strong" (v. 10). Accepting the thorns that God sees fit to keep
in our lives is the only way to find the strength that Paul is

talking about. Paul found Christ's strength working in him to be so powerful, so joy-producing, that he came to see his troubles—and they were many—as friends. Can we say like Paul, "I am content with weaknesses, insults, hardships, persecutions, and calamities"?

We can. We can be content with the thorns God allows if we shift our thinking to view them as opportunities. Each difficulty that comes our way, all that weakens us, is a fresh chance to cling to Christ and discover his power, his strength, and all that he is for us in the provision of himself. There are things about our union with Christ that we just cannot know apart from the thorns that spear our lives. That's why, when Paul had prayed for relief, Christ replied, "My grace is sufficient for you."

Is the grace of Christ sufficient for you too? You'll never know if you spend all your energy seeking to pull the thorn out of your flesh. If it's relief that you want—real relief—the kind that fills you with contentment, stop fighting when God says no. Listen instead to Christ's words to Paul, because they are his words to you as well.

Taking the Edge Off

*Any one of the house of Israel who takes his idols
into his heart and sets the stumbling block of his
iniquity before his face, and yet comes to the prophet,
I the LORD will answer him as he comes with the
multitude of his idols, that I may lay hold
of the hearts of the house of Israel,
who are all estranged from me through their idols.*

EZEKIEL 14:4–5

*H*ow do we find peace at the end of a pressure-filled day? The best thing to do, of course, is to find a quiet place to pray, to lift up our concerns and cast our cares upon God. But often that is not what we do. We seek escape instead. When life is particularly stressful, we find ourselves craving something—anything—that will obliterate our anxiety or at least take the edge off. So we dig into the chocolate or the chips. Or perhaps we get lost in mindless sitcoms. We might crack open a bottle of wine. Maybe we head to the mall or go shopping online.

The problem with using life's little pleasures as life's big escapes is that before long we come to depend on those pleasures. We find ourselves enacting tiny, daily rituals around our pet enjoyments, which only intensify the hold they have on us—a hold we often don't recognize for a long time. A woman who finds stress release in chocolate might build into her routine a three-o'clock run to the candy machine. Over time she becomes resentful of any interference that disrupts that mid-afternoon chocolate fix. Another likes to relax with a glass of wine before dinner; she looks forward to it every day. Before long she stops attending Bible studies or other evening functions that would preclude her evening drink. We become prisoners to the very thing that initially provided our escape.

A three-o'clock chocolate bar doesn't seem like all that big of a deal. Why shouldn't we enjoy life's little pleasures in the midst of our crazy routines? Aren't such things gifts? Of course they are, but not when we use them to obliterate tension or boredom or depression. When we turn life's little pleasures into remedies for life's troubles, we are setting up idols in our hearts, which actually push God aside. When a woman makes a bag of chips a habitual quick fix, according to God she "separates [herself] from me, taking [her] idols into [her] heart" (v. 7).

All idols are governed by the law of diminishing returns. The more we seek solace in our escape of choice, the farther from God we take ourselves and the more miserable we get. Eventually one chocolate bar won't be enough; we're going to want that after-dinner candy too. One glass of wine won't take the edge off forever; eventually two will be necessary. So how do we cope with those especially hard places, the situations we find so very difficult to cope with? The way *out* of the stress, the boredom, the loneliness, the depression, the fear, and the anxiety is found only by going *through* it. But we don't have to go it alone. Jesus tells us, "Come to me, all who labor and are heavy laden, and I will give you rest. Take my yoke upon you, and learn from me, for I am gentle and lowly in heart, and you will find rest for your souls. For my yoke is easy, and my burden is light" (Matt. 11:28–30).

A Woman's Pearls

*"Again, the kingdom of heaven is like a merchant in search
of fine pearls, who, on finding one pearl of great value,
went and sold all that he had and bought it."*

MATTHEW 13:45-46

*W*hat fine pearl are you searching for? Perhaps it's a
spouse or maybe an improvement on the spouse you have.
Maybe it's a new job, a bigger house, or successful children.
There are many wonderful gifts and blessings to be had, and
we want to lay hold of as many of them as we can. Inevitably,
though, there are some we don't get. Most of us live with
disappointment in our hearts concerning one or more of our
personal pearls. The pearl of marriage just never came along,
or if it did, it turned out to be a pearl with little luster. The
pearl of great talent never found an outlet; something or
someone came along and took away the opportunity to use
it. Or despite the care and diligence devoted to maintaining
the pearl of good health, it remains elusive.

There is only one pearl worth living for—the kingdom
of heaven. And from Jesus' parable we see that getting hold
of it is worth everything else we have. We nod our heads in
agreement, but do we really believe it? And something else
to consider: is this the pearl we really want? If we do, we

will invest our lives in it. Jesus tells us that God's kingdom is greater than any treasure, any blessing, anything else we will ever know. It is worth whatever it may cost us.

As Christians, Jesus' words sound good and right to us, and we want to feel this way. But we just don't. *Maybe I'll get there one day*, we think, *but today that's not where I'm at.* We believe that a wholehearted pursuit of the pearl of God's kingdom is something that only super-spiritual people are capable of, and we know we are a long way from that. So we trickle forward much as we have been, enjoying the occasional really good quiet time, seeking to trust God with our daily stresses, and just hoping that no big crisis comes along to knock the bottom out from under us. We settle for quasi-commitment, which produces quasi-contentment.

Many of us settle for that, though it is a far cry from the picture that Jesus paints of what can be ours right now, today. But actually it is possible to desire God so much that everything else pales in comparison. Such a yearning rarely happens overnight, but it can happen hour by hour, day by day. Each little difficulty gives us an opportunity to develop it. As we face today's disappointment, sin struggle, frustration, discouragement, or life-threatening crisis, we can go one of two ways. We can steel ourselves against it and fight our way out, or we can open up and let God into it. Each and every time something threatens to steal our peace, we can stop what we are doing and open that raw, painful place to God. Sometimes a brief but honest prayer is all we can manage. As often as possible, we do well to sit with his Word open before us, asking him to reveal himself in our struggle. The more we see, the more we will want. Before we know it, we will find ourselves wanting him even more than we want our problems solved. He himself will be the peace we have been wanting all along. He is faithful to us in this way. It has been said, and truthfully so, that sometimes we don't know God is all we have until God is all we've got.

Triumph in Tragedy

There came another and said, "Your sons and daughters
were eating and drinking wine in their oldest brother's house,
and behold, a great wind came across the wilderness
and struck the four corners of the house, and it fell upon
the young people, and they are dead, and I alone
have escaped to tell you." Then Job arose and tore his robe
and shaved his head and fell on the ground and worshiped.
And he said, "Naked I came from my mother's womb,
and naked shall I return. The LORD gave, and the LORD
has taken away; blessed be the name of the LORD."

JOB 1:18-21

*T*wo weeks ago, an expectant mother-to-be came by for a
visit. Although uncomfortable in the late-summer heat during her final days of pregnancy, Jalyn was bubbly and filled
with joy at the baby to come. She and her husband, already
blessed with a boy, were doubly excited because the new baby
was to be a girl.

Now, just a few minutes ago, I received word that Jalyn's
baby has died, just three days before the due date. At this
moment she is being induced to deliver the lifeless child.

"Why, God, why?" we are tempted to cry. "Where are you in this heartbreak?"

We don't know why. But we do know God was there: "For you formed my inward parts; you knitted me together in my mother's womb. . . . My frame was not hidden from you, when I was being made in secret, intricately woven in the depths of the earth. Your eyes saw my unformed substance; in your book were written, every one of them, the days that were formed for me, when as yet there was none of them" (Ps. 139:13, 15–16). Today Jalyn has tasted what Job did, pain that many of us will never know, pain from which some never recover. Those hit with such heartbreak can't imagine tasting joy ever again. But because Jalyn's faith is strong, I believe she will.

She has the kind of faith that leads to joy even in the most painful tragedies. She has the kind of faith that, even when tried in the hottest furnace, doesn't charge God with wrong. Such faith doesn't question his motives, doubt his kindness, or stop believing. And people with faith like Jalyn's and Job's do more than simply hang on—they reach out in their faith with praise, even while they weep.

Praise at a time like this goes against every fiber of our being. It just seems so contrary to the painful reality. But it is the only way back. It is the only way to triumph in tragedy. Praising God in the midst of life's worst devastations is actually not a contradiction because whatever he does is worthy of praise, even when it makes no sense to us. The death of a baby certainly isn't praiseworthy in itself, but the divine purposes that orchestrated it are indeed. Everything that befalls us is ordained by God; so we are right to praise him in all things. Because Jalyn knows herself to be one of

God's covenant children, she knows that God has no harmful intentions toward her; in fact, through the death of her baby he has plans to bless her. And she believes this, even before she sees how, even while she grieves.

A few weeks ago, the father of this unborn baby received a telephone call from friends, distraught parents who had returned home from an evening out to find the lifeless body of their eldest son, who had taken his own life. The expectant father rushed to their home, and after calling the police, he talked to the devastated parents about God's goodness.

The father-to-be has been hit with tragedy again today, but this time it's personal. But his convictions won't change because his faith in God's goodness is rock-solid. Shortly after learning that his unborn child had died, he was reminded of something he'd told the other grieving parents on the horrible night of their son's suicide: "The curtain to eternity is . . . torn back in the midst of tragedy to reveal our Savior."

The Lord gives, and he takes away. Blessed be his name because Christ is thereby revealed. Without the taking, we might not see him.

Safe, Secure, and Totally Bored

*Though the fig tree should not blossom, nor fruit be on
the vines, the produce of the olive fail and the fields yield
no food, the flock be cut off from the fold and there be no herd
in the stalls, yet I will rejoice in the LORD; I will take joy
in the God of my salvation. GOD, the Lord, is my strength;
he makes my feet like the deer's; he makes me tread
on my high places."*

HABAKKUK 3:17–19

*G*uaranteed to make you thin in just three weeks!"
"Lifetime warranty on all our merchandise."

"If your pizza isn't there in thirty minutes or less, it's free!"

Providing guarantees is a must for merchants in today's marketplace. We are suspicious of any product or service that doesn't come with a warranty. Trust extends no further than the terms of the guarantee. It's the American way.

A woman today who desires to emulate the home economics skills of the Proverbs 31 woman does her research: "She considers a field and buys it; with the fruit of her hands she plants a vineyard" (Prov. 31:16). Such a woman reads *Consumer Reports* magazine and scours all fine print for terms and conditions. That's just good common sense. The mistake we make is trying to apply the same principles to the Christian life.

"I feel called to go to the mission field, but I don't know if that's wise financially."

"Tom has asked me to marry him, and he seems to be a godly man. I'm just so afraid of marrying the wrong person."

We don't want to trust God; we want a guarantee that things will work out in our favor, and we hesitate to make a move without one. So we take no risks; we settle for what we know because what we don't know is just too scary. We accept the trade-off—an underlying dissatisfaction—so we can stay safe. The American way has led to unhappiness in the Christian life for many of us today.

Going to the mission field *is* financially risky; there are no guarantees of a nice, fat pension upon retirement. When we choose a marriage partner, we are choosing not to have whatever other option might come along down the road. Christ offered no guarantees of the sort that make us comfortable. The fig tree may never blossom; the flock may never return to the fold.

Desiring to know the outcome of our choices is only natural, which is why Peter asked Jesus, "We have left everything and followed you. What then will we have?" (Matt. 19:27). Jesus replied that those who leave all to follow him will indeed be blessed for doing so and will ultimately lack nothing. But we want the details of those blessings in advance; we want guaranteed specifics.

There is only one absolute guarantee for Christians, and it is this: "For those who love God all things work together for good, for those who are called according to his purpose.

For those whom he foreknew he also predestined to be conformed to the image of his Son, in order that he might be the
firstborn among many brothers" (Rom. 8:28–29).

That is why we can step out on a risky course, if God calls
us to do so. It's why Habakkuk could rejoice with no figs,
no fruit, no olives, no flocks, and no herds in the stalls. God
was his strength, and he is ours. We may have no guarantees
that the things we hope for will come, but God will do for
us what he did for Habakkuk—lead us to life in the highest
places with him, no matter where it takes us, no matter what
we leave behind.

What We Ask For

They soon forgot His works; they did not wait for
His counsel, but lusted exceedingly in the wilderness,
and tested God in the desert. And He gave them
their request, but sent leanness into their soul.

PSALM 106:13–15 NKJV

*D*esire without restraint is a dangerous thing. It is obsession. If we set our hope exclusively on something we want, before long we won't be satisfied with anything else. When obtaining the object of our desire becomes the thing we live for, God and his ways fall lower and lower on our priority list and eventually get pushed out entirely. We no longer approach God in his Word with a listening heart. Yet we don't realize we aren't really listening because our hearts are so set on the thing we want. We find out only later, when things have gone terribly wrong.

Gwen found that out a few years ago when she got involved with a man she met over the Internet. After several months of online conversations, she and Brian decided to meet, and their first date was every bit as wonderful as they had anticipated. Once they met face-to-face, their relationship developed quickly. But as the months passed, Gwen felt increasingly depressed. Brian frequently made jokes at her expense, little offhand comments that cut her down in front of others. Brian also kept much of his life hidden from Gwen. He was evasive about his activities when he wasn't with her. He also had constant excuses for missing church, and despite his profession of faith, there was little evidence that Gwen could see to back up that profession. Her friends didn't seem to like Brian very much, and they cautioned Gwen about allowing herself to become more deeply involved. Gwen finally shared all of this with her pastor, who strongly advised her against proceeding with the relationship.

But Gwen didn't stop. Despite the clear warnings from her friends and her pastor, despite her diminishing sense of joy when in Brian's company, and despite the fact that Brian lacked the godly qualities she had always wanted in a husband, she married him. And one year later he left her.

So much of the heartache we bring on ourselves comes from the fact that we are set on getting something that God is clearly not blessing for one reason or another. If we are walking closely with God, it is quite easy to recognize if his hand is not in it. He is gracious, and I have yet to see a situation in which he had failed to provide sufficient warnings. Gwen wanted marriage so badly that she "soon forgot His works"; she "did not wait for His counsel, but lusted exceedingly in the wilderness, and tested God in the desert." And just as God had done with the Israelites, he gave Gwen her request but "sent leanness into [her] soul."

The incident on which Psalm 106 is based occurred when God's people, the Israelites, were wandering in the wilderness. After months of seemingly pointless journeying, they were understandably tired of the desert. Wildernesses, by definition, are difficult places. They are barren places, lacking one or more of the comforts for which we long.

Wildernesses are many and varied. Some of us know the wilderness of singleness. Others know the wilderness of unemployment, or the bad health wilderness, or the difficult marriage wilderness. Wildernesses are places we long to leave. That is exactly how Gwen had felt. More than anything she wanted to get out of the singleness desert and into what she saw as the promised land of marriage, and the more she focused on the difficulty of her wilderness, the less she focused on God until finally her desire for escape and pleasure grew so big that God became small in her heart.

How do we handle our wildernesses? Are we willing to live contentedly with God's provision for us in them, or are we so set on something we want him to give us that we stop trusting, stop waiting, stop listening? Nothing good will come from allowing ourselves to be ruled by what we lack in the wilderness, and often what we do manage to lay hold of will taste bitter when we get it. Sometimes God gives us what we want to show us what we need. What Gwen really needed was not a husband. It was to wait in the wilderness of singleness until or unless a biblical opportunity for marriage came along. If she had not been so fixated on her desire, she would have been able to see that marrying Brian was biblically unwise.

God determines the length of our wilderness wanderings according to his own purposes, and those purposes always include our long-term benefit, which we will see if we just wait for him. Belief that God has our good in mind now, not just on the other side of the desert, is what we need, and it is the way to live contentedly in a difficult situation when we can see no end in sight. Contentment comes by believing that we have everything we need for today. God hasn't left one single thing out. If we needed it, we would have it, and therefore what we do have today is all we need. Do you believe that? Just as importantly, do you accept it? If so, you will get to experience the joy of contentment even before your prayer for a particular blessing has been answered.

Dreams Come True

*Delight yourself in the LORD, and he will give you
the desires of your heart.*

PSALM 37:4

*W*e all have desires, certain things we believe will bring us
the happiness for which we so deeply yearn. So when we first
encounter David's words here in Psalm 37 our hopes soar. At
last! We believe we have found the way to make our dreams
come true. We simply have to ask God to give us what we
long for, and he will do so.

His character is certainly one that delights to bless, but he
knows that many of the things for which we long won't turn
out quite the way we imagine. God can see the downsides
that we cannot, which is why some of the things we want
most desperately and pray for most intently do not come to
pass. That's why we cannot interpret David's word as a blank
check from heaven, and if we do, sooner or later we are going
to be disillusioned.

Happiness is promised in this verse, but not in the way
we might first think. There are actually two wonderful ways
we can rightly apply these words in Psalm 37. First, when
we center our affections, our pursuits, and everything about
ourselves on Christ, something amazing happens. He actu-

ally plants within us desires for things that he desires for us. Someone wisely said, "We are conformed to that upon which we center our interest and love." Our desires, therefore, if centered on God and his ways, are going to be conformed to his desires for us.

Because we are sinful, we will never be completely sure whether our desires spring from God or from our flesh. In this lifetime even our best, most God-centered desires are going to be tainted by sin. But in orienting ourselves around Christ, we are much more likely to desire the things he longs to give and therefore see more of our dreams come true.

The second way we can rightly apply the promise of Psalm 37:4 is that the more we seek Christ, the better we will know him, and the more we know him, the more of him we will want to know and possess and treasure. He himself is the ultimate fulfillment of our desires. Seek your happiness in the Lord, and he will give you the desires of your heart—he will give you himself. Does this seem unreal or impossible to you? Are you tempted to think these are just the words of David on a spiritually good day? Don't be afraid or ashamed of your desire to be happy. Instead, take it to God; seek it in him. You will find that David's words are really and truly God's promise to you.

Blaise Pascal (1623–1662) wrote, "All men seek happiness. This is without exception. Whatever different means they employ, they all tend to this end. The cause of some going to war, and of others avoiding it, is the same desire in both, attended with different views. The will never takes the least step but to this object. This is the motive of every action of every man, even of those who hang themselves."

John Piper builds on Pascal's words with some important biblical truth:

> Does seeking your own happiness sound self-centered? Aren't Christians supposed to seek God, not their own pleasure? To answer this question we need to understand a crucial truth about pleasure-seeking (hedonism): *we value most what we delight in most*. Pleasure is not God's competitor, idols are. Pleasure is simply a gauge that measures how valuable someone or something is to us. Pleasure is the measure of our treasure. . . . Nowhere in the Bible does God condemn people for longing to be happy. People are condemned for forsaking God and seeking their happiness elsewhere (Jeremiah 2:13).[1]

That is why happiness, the dream-come-true kind of happiness, is possible right now, today.

---

[1] John Piper, http://www.desiringgod.org/AboutUs/OurDistinctives/ChristianHedonism/; emphasis in original.

Settling Down

*"You shall love the Lord your God with all your heart
and with all your soul and with all your mind.
This is the great and first commandment.
And a second is like it: You shall love your neighbor
as yourself. On these two commandments
depend all the Law and the Prophets."*

MATTHEW 22:37-40

Starting over is never easy, but some of us do a lot of it. We move from job to job, church to church, relationship to relationship, and every time we uproot we leave behind established routines and relationships. Resettling into something new is often a long, lonely process. So why do we do it? Some of the changes we make are necessary. We lose our job or our spouse walks out or a family member becomes ill. Many of us, however, change our lives solely because we get restless. Whether or not we recognize it, we are on a quest for the next thing, the newest excitement, or just something different from the routine. We undertake yet another upheaval because we are addicted to change. Loneliness is the inevitable result, and when we can't fill up the emptiness in a short time, we hit the road again in search of something or someone to fill the void.

What we don't recognize easily is that our discontentment, our restlessness, does not come from the fact that we lack something we need; because we don't see that, we believe fulfillment is right around the corner, at the next job, in the next church, with the next relationship. That is what drives us to keep moving. The loneliness that results from such a life is very real and certainly breeds discontentment. But the solution is not to be found in yet another new place.

We are actually lonely and discontent because we are refusing to invest. We aren't giving ourselves fully to God and to the relationships we have today. We are so busy looking for fulfillment and meaning that we miss it altogether. We simply do not see that purpose and contentment come from giving up ourselves rather than giving up everything and everyone else.

Investing in God and in people is to invest in happiness, because investing is what God has designed us for and called us to. That is why discarding people and places in a search for happiness is actually to forfeit the very thing we have been looking for. Love—the giving of ourselves to God and to those he has placed around us—and contentment go hand in hand. If we will just stop searching and start investing, we will find the sort of happiness that will slay our restlessness.

Lingering Looks

Lot's wife, behind him, looked back, and
she became a pillar of salt.

GENESIS 19:26

As morning dawned, the angels urged Lot, saying, "Up! Take your wife and your two daughters who are here, lest you be swept away in the punishment of the city" (v. 15). Guidance doesn't get much clearer than that. God was leading Lot and his family away from their home, out of the city of Sodom. But Lot, his wife, and his two daughters were reluctant to leave; they were well established in the community of Sodom. So despite the ungodliness all around them, despite the angels' warnings about the destruction that was about to fall on the community, they hesitated.

It seems to make no sense. The wise choice was obvious—go! But they lingered because their hearts were centered on what they enjoyed in Sodom. Lot, along with his wife and daughters, had come to enjoy a measure of social prestige in that community. Nevertheless, God didn't allow this harmful focus to destroy their lives: "So the men seized him and his wife and his two daughters by the hand, the LORD being merciful to him, and they brought him out and set him outside the city" (v. 16). Lot's wife, however, was so centered on her life in Sodom that her heart was tuned out to God and his goodness to her. She looked back toward Sodom and lost her life.

Looking backward—it's something we are all tempted to do from time to time. For some of us, as was the case with Lot's wife, it is the company of worldly people and material pleasures that we miss, especially when living the Christian life costs us things we might enjoy otherwise. But often our backward look isn't so much to worldly gain as it is simply to a time that worked a little better than today. Perhaps now we do not enjoy the same quality of friendships that we knew before, or perhaps the teaching and worship in our new church isn't quite what we'd like. When life is lacking, we are prone to look back; and if our look is a lingering one, we are liable to wind up in trouble.

If we focus overly much on what we *had* rather than on what we *have*, we are sowing seeds of discontent, and once discontentment sets in, we may find ourselves pondering, *Maybe I should never have left. Maybe I should go back.* We become consumed with regaining a time in our lives that "worked." Now, sometimes going back is the answer. We cannot discount the possibility that, unlike Lot and his family, it was our leaving that was wrong rather than our staying. But more often than not, this isn't the case. And regardless of why we left, we are where we are today by God's providence. "The heart of man plans his way, but the LORD establishes his steps" (Prov. 16:9). Whether our leaving was right or wrong, finding our way back to happiness does not begin with packing our bags.

The changes we make in our lives usually stem from our desires for one or more of the things that we see in front of us—more fulfilling work, a better quality of life, more intimate relationships. When our lives change, some things will be better than what we had before; other aspects of life will not. If we set our minds on acquiring what is still missing, we will get caught up in comparing and contrasting the old and the new, and we will determine that we must keep going until we have it all, because, we reason, if we don't have it all, we haven't yet found where God wants us to be. So we leave one place—a job, a church, or a relationship—for yet another in hope of something better, only to find that we still aren't satisfied.

Regaining our peace begins with the realization that God does not guide our steps for the sole purpose of blessing our earthly lot. If we are under the illusion that God moved us in order to better our circumstances but things go badly, we are going to think that somewhere along the way we missed his guidance. Obtaining earthly ease is not primarily why God shifts our lives around. All God does in our lives and everywhere he leads us has one overarching purpose, which is to deepen our relationship with him and to further his glory through us. All other blessings we get in the process are just gravy. Fulfilling work, like-minded friends, and a nice house are extras. These are God's blessings, not his purposes, in his leading of our lives.

No matter where we are today or how we got here, we are here because God brought us to this place in our lives so that we might enjoy him more fully and bring glory to Christ. Contentment is to be found right where we are, and we will lay hold of it when we thank him for his wise providence in leading us here, even if we cannot see how his primary purpose is playing out just yet. "Thank you, God, that I am in this place, in this job, in this marriage because for reasons I cannot understand, it is benefiting my relationship with you and is pointing me and others toward Christ."

A heartfelt grasp of God's primary purpose will enable us to enjoy his secondary blessings and also to live contentedly with those we lack. Once we grasp this, maybe then we will determine to stay put. Or maybe we will go back. Whatever we choose to do, we will see that happiness doesn't hinge on which way we go.

Made Ready for Anything

"Go your way. Eat the fat and drink sweet wine and
send portions to anyone who has nothing ready,
for this day is holy to our Lord. And do not be grieved,
for the joy of the LORD is your strength."

NEHEMIAH 8:10

I just can't see how I can do it!" Natalie told her Bible
study group. "It's overwhelming to think about. We've got
five teenagers! How can Jim's mother possibly come live with
us? I know it's the right thing to do. God calls us to take care
of our family members, but my mother in law, Betty, and I
have never had an easy relationship as it is! What will it be
like living under the same roof?"

Sometimes God calls us to do hard things. Natalie is facing one of those right now. She and Jim have talked it over
and spent much time praying about the best way to provide
for Betty. It has become increasingly apparent that she needs
assisted care. Although the Bible doesn't spell out how to
care for Betty, God's Word is clear—providing care for aging
parents is a part of what Christians are called to do.

After exploring a variety of options, the best thing seems
to be bringing Betty out West to live with them. Jim is rightly
concerned about how the proposed living arrangement might

impact Natalie and their marriage; he knows that although caring for his mother is right, his marriage is meant to hold a higher priority. So Jim is willing to defer to Natalie. He has left the choice to her, which is what she is now discussing with her Bible study group.

Despite Natalie's anxious reservations, she wants to show love to her husband and her mother-in-law, and most of all she wants to please God. For those reasons, she has already made up her mind, and she is planning to tell Jim to invite Betty. What she is still dealing with today at Bible study is how, having made the decision, she can possibly live with it.

We all face dilemmas of one sort or another, choices in which the most loving and biblical path will require a measure of discomfort on our part. Some of us find ourselves in this very position today. How do we go forward into difficulties such as Natalie's without a constant undercurrent of dread or irritation? We do so by getting to the root of what is causing our distasteful feelings about our circumstances and then bringing God's Word to bear on that root.

In Natalie's case the root of her concern is her role as homemaker. She quite naturally values her home and family life; she loves managing her domestic realm and caring for her family. At the root of her anxiety is the fear that once Betty comes under her roof, some of this will be taken away from her. But Natalie has nothing to dread if she will allow God, rather than her role in her home, to be the source of her joy.

We can face anything, even the most unpalatable circumstances, if we look to God as our source of happiness. No matter what we are dealing with, God is there overseeing, loving, providing. "God is our refuge and strength, a very present help in trouble" (Ps. 46:1). Sometimes the very reason he leads us into difficulty is just so we will discover how much joy is to be found in the shadow of his wings. Natalie, and we, too, in our unique trials, will find something else as well—strength to do what seems impossible. The joy we find in the Lord actually produces strength in us to do the impossible.

Are you facing an impossible situation today? If so, contrary as it seems, rejoice in the Lord. Rejoicing, the activity of joy, begins with offering him thanks—even about the very thing we are dreading. When we do so, we are acknowledging his good hand in it, even when we cannot yet see the good that he has in store. Begin with thanks, and joy will soon follow. So will the strength we need to face our circumstances with a happiness we never thought possible.

Let's Not Kid Ourselves

For when I kept silent, my bones wasted away
through my groaning all day long. For day and night
your hand was heavy upon me; my strength was dried up
as by the heat of summer.

PSALM 32:3-4

That little indulgence, the small undercurrent of bitterness, the well-masked dislike of our neighbor—are these really such a big deal? "I'm just not quite ready to pull that out and look at it," we decide, "and God's grace covers it anyway." But such thinking is dangerous. All of our sins are really much worse than we think. There are no little sins in God's eyes, and to think otherwise is to abuse his grace. When the Lord puts his finger on a particular sin we are tolerating, and we choose to continue in it, backing up our choice with the truth that "where sin increased, grace abounded all the more" (Rom. 5:20), we are abusing grace.

God, who is both loving and holy, will not allow us to continue the abuse for long. Sooner or later the weight of unrepentant sin presses down heavily upon us. If we aren't ready to deal with the sin, we are going to look everywhere else for an explanation about that pressing.

"I'm just irritable this week because my hormones are out of whack."

"I've been so blue for the past few weeks. I just can't shake it. I think I need a vacation. All work and no play . . ."

"My quiet times haven't been so good lately. I'm having trouble connecting with God. It must be because I'm super-busy. Things will quiet down in a week or two, and then I'll set aside some time to be in the Word."

We certainly harm ourselves and grieve God when we falter under a weight of guilt, worrying that the most trivial of annoyances and every bad mood must be a result of unconfessed sin, which is to ignore grace altogether. But our tendency is to err in the other direction, making too little of our sin rather than too much. "Much sickness—physical, mental, and emotional—surely must come from disobedience," writes Elisabeth Elliot. "When the soul is confronted with an alternative of right or wrong and chooses to blur the distinction, making excuses for its bewilderment and frustration, it is exposed to infection."[1]

God is faithful, and he will not allow us to abuse grace indefinitely. He cares too much about his glory and the trifling we are doing with Christ's sacrifice for us. He also knows that when we insist on keeping our little secret sins we are erecting a wedge in our relationship with him. Have you been unhappy lately? If so, have you examined your heart and your life to see if you are tolerating something that displeases God, however small it may seem? We are so quick to discount the impact of unrepentant sin on our moods and circumstances, largely because we don't want our secret sins to be the underlying cause. We look for every other possible

[1]Elisabeth Elliot, *Discipline: The Glad Surrender* (Grand Rapids, MI: Revell, 1982), 74.

cause first and make small tweaks to our lives and routines in an attempt to regain our contentment.

Finding out that your unhappiness is caused by unrepentant sin is not as hard to discover as you might think. It's simple, really. First, is there something you are tolerating in your life in clear violation of Scripture, or are you twisting Scripture to fit your desires, choosing to blur the edges of what constitutes obedience? Second, is your conscience troubled, however much you may have excused it? If so, pray about it. Bounce it off your pastor or a godly friend. Our consciences aren't always reliable guides, but if there is pressing weight there, something somewhere is surely off base. Jonathan Edwards said, "A man never, in any instance, wills anything contrary to his desires." If we are attempting to make peace with sin, no matter how trivial, we can count on the fact that sooner or later God is going to deal with it.

Before you make adjustments to your life or run to the doctor for a new medication or point the finger at someone else, deal with that thing, that one little thing, you have been discounting as no big deal. Take it to God; be willing to pull it out into the open before him; tell him of your willingness to deal with it in the strength he will give you to do so. You'll find contentment coming back into your soul, even before you have gotten up from your knees. That's what David, the author of Psalm 32, did, and this is what he found:

> I acknowledged my sin to you,
>   and I did not cover my iniquity;
> I said, "I will confess my transgressions to the LORD,"
>   and you forgave the iniquity of my sin. Selah

Therefore let everyone who is godly
   offer prayer to you at a time when you may be found;
surely in the rush of great waters,
   they shall not reach him.
You are a hiding place for me;
   you preserve me from trouble;
   you surround me with shouts of deliverance. Selah *(vv. 5–7)*

Our Vital Need for Hope

I would have lost heart, unless I had believed that I would see the goodness of the LORD in the land of the living."

PSALM 27:13, NKJV

*C*ontentment is a choice, although at times it is hard to believe that. It just makes no sense. We would give anything to get out of the funk in which we find ourselves. But picking ourselves up by our purse straps isn't going to do it. We need an answer; we need help. And if we do not get it, what starts out as a mild case of the blues can spiral down into depression, which leads to discouragement, and then finally to despair. There is a common thread in each slide we make down this awful spiral—a loss of hope. Each time we move a little lower, it is because a little more hope has died.

The apostle Paul wrote, "So now faith, hope, and love abide, these three; but the greatest of these is love" (1 Cor. 13:13). Since his words occur in a section of his letter that focuses on love, we often overlook the faith and hope part, but each aspect of this trio is of vital importance to our walk with God and to our spiritual and emotional sanity. If we are struggling with contentment, is there a corresponding loss of hope in our hearts? So long as hope remains alive, we are all right.

The key, of course, to not losing hope is to place our hope in the right things. If we set our hope on something—even a very good something—that we want in this life, we may well lose our hope because there are no guarantees that we will get the things we want in the here and now. There is only one thing of which we can be sure, and that is God's presence and all the blessings that come with it. Our hope will find increasing fulfillment if what we hope for is to know more of Christ. Our hopes will be realized if deeper intimacy with our heavenly Father is what we seek. Our hopes will not disappoint if we long to be free of our enslaving sins. We can bank our hopes on any and all of the things God has promised us in his Word. Paul had the right idea about hope fulfilled when he prayed "that the God of our Lord Jesus Christ, the Father of glory, may give you a spirit of wisdom and of revelation in the knowledge of him, having the eyes of your hearts enlightened, that you may know what is the hope to which he has called you, what are the riches of his glorious inheritance in the saints" (Eph. 1:17–18).

But that doesn't mean we have to give up on having answers to our prayers for our more mundane concerns. Far from it! We have a God who delights to bless us, and one of the ways he reveals his character is by showing us that he is adequate to meet our needs and by demonstrating that he has heard the deep cries of our hearts. It is good and right to hope for God's answers to our prayers for all things. David had just such hope, which is why he didn't fall to discouragement in hard times. Look at what James Boice said about David's words in Psalm 27:

David is not speaking about the afterlife here. He is speaking about "the land of the living," here and now. But . . . the things he is praying for (and for which we pray) do not always come to us at once. God has his timings, which are not ours, and therefore what we pray for and need is sometimes delayed. What then? Are we to despair of having answers, to lose confidence? Not at all! We simply need to wait.[1]

We pour ourselves into growing our faith and our love. Let's not forget hope. Don't let its spark die out. Fight for it, pray for it, and set it on God himself ahead of everything else. To choose hope is to choose contentment.

---

[1]James Boice, *Psalms 1–41* (Grand Rapids, MI: Baker, 1994), 1:243.

Going Without

*I rejoice in my sufferings for your sake, and
in my flesh I am filling up what is lacking in Christ's
afflictions for the sake of his body, that is, the church.*

COLOSSIANS 1:24

The apostle Paul certainly understood suffering. He was abused, beaten, rejected, and homeless, all because he took a very public stand for Christ. When we hear about Paul and people like him, we rightly hesitate to apply the word *suffering* to much of what we classify as difficult in our lives. Many of our trials seem so trivial in comparison, and in truth many of them are. Yet recognizing the truth of the comparison doesn't help us very much when we hurt. We are not going to feel better simply by acknowledging that Paul had it worse. But there is something about his suffering that can help us deal with our own.

Paul said that he actually rejoiced in his sufferings. How can that be? He rejoiced because he saw his sufferings as a way to represent Christ to others. That is what he meant by "filling up what is lacking in Christ's afflictions." Christ's whole life on earth was one of suffering, and now that he was no longer in the world, Paul, through his sufferings, had opportunities to stand in Christ's place. He rejoiced in his sufferings because living with them was something he could do for his beloved Savior. To Paul's way of thinking, suffering really was a privilege.

I marvel at Paul, don't you? Honestly, who among us thinks the way he did? Perhaps some of us do; many more do not. But we can if we make Christ our goal in life. We'll find then that we actually think more like Paul than we ever thought possible. Ironically, rejoicing is sometimes easier in the bigger crises. That's because it is during such times that we tend to know that extra measure of strength and grace, the comfort in affliction that we are promised in God's Word. Paul wrote, "Blessed be the God and Father of our Lord Jesus Christ, the Father of mercies and God of all comfort, who comforts us in all our affliction, so that we may be able to comfort those who are in any affliction, with the comfort with which we ourselves are comforted by God" (2 Cor. 1:3–4).

Yet the less life-shattering trials, those we hesitate to call suffering but require us to do spiritual and emotional battle every day, give us just as much opportunity to find the blessing Paul is talking about here.

The single woman who wants to be married but sees no prospect on the horizon; the couple who longs for a child but cannot conceive; the woman who is married to an unbeliever and attends church alone every Sunday. These are forms of suffering, but if we can think of nothing except escaping our situation, over time situations such as these are going to wear us down and discourage our faith. Yet it is in these very sorts of sufferings that we have tremendous opportunity, because people are watching us. My unbelieving family members watch how I handle my singleness. Am I going to complain bitterly about it and spend all my time and effort trying to find a mate? If so, I will miss an opportunity to demonstrate that God is trustworthy and kind and faithful, something I can only do by believing that God is really all those things, even when it includes singleness. Childless couples and lonely wives have the same opportunity. People are watching how you handle your pain. Hard as it is to embrace, the truth is that Christ is a lot more evident in how we handle our lack than in how we handle our gain.

If we are willing to suffer for this purpose—as ambassadors for Christ—we are going to find contentment in it, whether or not our difficulty changes tomorrow or the next day. Perhaps someone you love will come to faith tomorrow because of what they see in you today. And undoubtedly those around you who are suffering will be encouraged.

To whom do you turn when you want answers for life's painful mysteries? Most likely you seek out someone who has known suffering. At some level everyone realizes that bearing pain brings with it a degree of wisdom and insight that nothing else does. It is to this that we turn in our troubles, and it is to this—in us—to which others will turn in theirs. Through the issue we are laboring under, whatever it is, God is making us into instruments of wisdom and encouragement. That is a privilege, and recognizing it as such is the road to contentment whenever we are called to live in need.

A Sinful Swap

In any and every circumstance, I have learned the secret
of facing plenty and hunger, abundance and need.
I can do all things through him who strengthens me.

PHILIPPIANS 4:12-13

*D*esire for life's good gifts is natural. But there is a difference between desiring good things for the right reasons and desiring them simply because others have them. Our hearts are tricky and complex, and only God knows them accurately, but we can often discern what motivates our desires by watching for certain triggers. We are perfectly content with our condo until we visit Courtney's townhouse. We are content to be single until we watch Ginny fall in love and get engaged. We are content with a B+ on our essay until we learn that Samantha got an A. Desiring a nice home, a husband, and success in our work is good; wanting those things because we feel we are missing out is coveting.

Those of us aware of the dangers of coveting seek to avoid it, and one quick and easy way we are tempted to do so is by taking mental stock of everyone we can think of who has less than we do. In fact, we are often encouraged to do so by well-meaning friends:

"You may live in a small condo, but you have more space all to yourself than do most families worldwide."

"I'm sure your job gets boring sometimes, but at least you aren't unemployed like Amanda."

"Of course, I can understand that coming home to an empty house every night gets lonely, but at least you don't have to worry about cooking dinner for an entire family every night like Kris does."

While such comparisons are good and right in helping us count our blessings and foster a heart of gratitude, using them to feel good about our lives is really just swapping pride for covetousness. We engage in this swap when we seek to make ourselves feel better because someone lacks what we have. We don't see the apostles ever doing that. Paul, whose words on contentment largely shape our understanding of how to acquire it, never once suggests that we should be satisfied with what we have because others have less. He did not say, "In any and every circumstance, I have learned the secret of facing plenty and hunger, abundance and need. I can do all things because I have it better than Peter or James or John." His comparisons were never horizontal; they were always vertical. Christ was his source, his secret, of contentment.

We will always be able to point to people who are worse off than we are; likewise, there will always be those who have it better. So using comparison as a contentment control gauge is a zero-sum game. The reason we can live contentedly with unmet desires is because Christ will enable us to do so. He supplies from himself whatever we lack in the here and now. Something Paul does do is to make clear that contentment is something we learn. So if we are struggling to acquire it or to maintain the contentment we have already tasted, we must not be discouraged. It will grow over time as we seek it in biblical ways.

On the flipside, the strength of Christ is also the means to live well with desires fulfilled. Grace is necessary to avoid taking satisfaction in what we have that others lack. Even Paul had to learn how to be content with abundance: "In any and every circumstance, I have learned the secret of facing *plenty* and hunger, *abundance* and need." What he had learned since becoming a Christian was the truth that he deserved nothing; he had no right or claim to anything. The same is true of us, and once we realize it we too will no longer be oriented around the things we do not have because we will be so grateful for whatever we get.

Satisfaction Guaranteed

"Blessed are those who hunger and thirst for righteousness,
for they shall be satisfied."

Matthew 5:6

*T*here is a reason why the Rolling Stones 1965 hit "(I Can't Get No) Satisfaction" is number one on VH1's "100 Greatest Rock and Roll Songs of All Time."

> *I can't get no satisfaction,*
> *I can't get no satisfaction.*
> *'Cause I try and I try and I try and I try.*
> *I can't get no, I can't get no.*

The song's enduring popularity is due to the fact that it sums up the human condition. We try and we try and we try, yet we never find the satisfaction for which our souls long. But while that is truly the human condition, it is not the redeemed human condition. Satisfaction is readily available for anyone who knows where to look. Deep and enduring satisfaction is found only in Christ, and the satisfaction he gives is one we don't have to try and try and try to grasp hold of. It is readily supplied to all those who seek it in him.

We remain restless in our search for satisfaction because we set our sights too low. We pursue the perfect match—the

job, relationship, church, community, house—that is just
right for us. Sometimes we find it, only to realize in time that
it isn't quite the perfect match it seemed at first. So we get
back on the treadmill.

There is nothing sinful about the desire for fulfillment—
it is God-given! God created us to be satisfied, which is why
we hunger for it in the first place. But because we are sinful,
our tendency is to turn away from the one place where we
are meant to find it. The only way to be reconnected with
this one source of satisfaction is through Christ. It is in him
that we are united to God and made capable of experiencing
the fulfillment for which we were created. That is what Jesus
meant when he said that those who hunger and thirst for
righteousness will be filled.

The righteousness of which he spoke is not a legalistic
keeping of the rules. Jesus' words are not going to be very
appealing to us if we think he is talking about mustering up a
desire for a list of do's and don'ts. When he said, "Blessed are
those who hunger and thirst for righteousness," he was really
speaking about himself. He is our righteousness: "You are
in Christ Jesus, who became to us wisdom from God, *righteousness* and sanctification and redemption" (1 Cor. 1:30).
If we hunger and thirst for him, we are promised satisfaction.
Underneath it all, what we are really after is never the perfect
match; it's the satisfaction that we think such a match will
bring us. Satisfaction is what our hearts crave.

"Okay," you say, "all of this sounds good in theory, but
how do we actually get there?" If we are honest, we must
admit that we do not feel a hunger for Jesus quite as much as
we feel a hunger for other things. But the way there is really
not difficult at all. If we ask God to create in us a hunger

for Jesus, we can be sure that he will do so. In one way or another, he will begin to show us our need for Christ. One of the ways God does this is to expose us to ourselves. Once we get a glimpse of who we really are, believe me, we will be awakened to our need. God will also show us who he really is, and what we see can't help but draw us in. So ask him. Ask to see yourself through his eyes, and ask for a clearer glimpse of Christ. Hunger for God will surely grow.

But God doesn't sit back and wait for us to ask. The very fact that we hunger for satisfaction indicates that he is already working to that end in our hearts.

Filled to the Full

*The woman said to him, "Sir, give me this water,
so that I will not be thirsty or have to come here
to draw water."*

JOHN 4:15

*J*esus was sitting by a well one hot day when a woman
came to draw water. This was unusual. Women typically
came earlier in the morning, before the midday sun made
the task more difficult. Her timing was purposeful, however;
she waited until the others had long come and gone to avoid
their scorn. This woman was a social outcast. Her checkered
past was characterized by immorality, and her present wasn't
much better.

Jesus was waiting for her though. Meeting her was the
reason he had stopped at the well in the first place. He knew
she'd be coming. He also knew her deep desire for love and
security and acceptance. The woman had spent years in
her quest, always thirsting, never finding. By the time Jesus
found her, she had cycled through five husbands and was
now living with a man to whom she was not married. Her
solitary trip to the well is indicative of the shame she felt
about it all, yet her yearning held her captive to a lifestyle
of immorality.

Women today are not all that different in heart from this woman of Samaria. We, too, desire love, security, and a sense of belonging. Some of us have chosen the same path for fulfillment that she chose, and we have wound up in the same place—lonely and still thirsting. Perhaps you are one of them. Maybe right now, today, you are caught up in the cycle of attaching yourself to man after man in abject fear of being alone. Or if you are not in that place today, perhaps you were at one time, and the shame of your past keeps you isolated from real intimacy with anyone in the present. If so, Jesus comes to you in the same way he came to the woman of Samaria.

Jesus asked the woman for a drink, and she marveled that he would even speak to her. Not only was she a moral outcast, she was one of the despised Samaritans with whom Jews did not associate. But Jesus said to her, "If you knew the gift of God, and who it is that is saying to you, 'Give me a drink,' you would have asked him, and he would have given you living water . . . whoever drinks of the water that I will give him will never be thirsty again" (John 4:10, 14). That is all she had to do—just ask—and she would receive.

The woman did not understand what Jesus was really offering. She latched onto what he said just because she thought he was able to make her life a little bit easier. As do we! But Jesus had far more in mind to give her. He had come to set her free from her self-made prison by quenching the deep thirst in her heart that had done nothing so far but drive her entire life into the ground.

In order that she realize all he had for her, he exposed her deepest yearning to the light:

Jesus said to her, "Go, call your husband, and come here." The woman answered him, "I have no husband." Jesus said to her, "You are right in saying, 'I have no husband'; for you have had five husbands, and the one you now have is not your husband. What you have said is true." (vv. 16–18)

Where does your deepest yearning lie? Wherever it is, Jesus longs to meet you there, and it is there that you will find him.

He promised the Samaritan woman something that would satisfy in a way that nothing else had ever been able to do, and he promises the same to us. What are you searching for, and where are you looking? Everything you are looking for is all in one place.

Hungry Hearts

Jesus said to them, "I am the bread of life;
whoever comes to me shall not hunger, and
whoever believes in me shall never thirst."

JOHN 6:35

*W*hile HIV/AIDS, malaria, and hosts of other diseases flourish in underprivileged countries, bulimia, one of the ugliest plagues of all time, proliferates in the privileged West. It can only flourish in places of abundance because one aspect of bulimia involves gorging on massive quantities of food. Someone I know who has battled bulimia for years told me, "I live in fear of ever feeling empty." Why, in a country where food is so plentiful, would she harbor such a fear? She is mistaking spiritual emptiness for physical hunger. Many have labeled bulimia a disease, and they are right—it is sin, and sin is disease of the soul.

Bulimia, like all sin, is the attempt to find satisfaction apart from God. Sins such as this may provide a quick fix, an escape from stress, unhappiness, and the angst of life, but the fix is short-lived; empty reality is right there waiting to assume its overarching place. That is what my friend is so afraid of. She is desperate to get away from the emptiness of life, but she can never quite accomplish that. Escape is not what she needs. What she and all of us need is something to assuage our soul hunger.

Christ is the answer, as we who are Christians realize. But we are kidding ourselves if we think bulimia and related sins affect only those outside the church. It is rampant inside, too. The reason is that although we are looking to Christ, many of us are looking to him for fulfillment of the wrong kind. That is exactly what the hungry crowd was doing the day Jesus fed them with five barley loaves and two fish. The five thousand ate their fill, and afterward they wanted to be Jesus' followers. But to some of them he said, "Truly, truly, I say to you, you are seeking me, not because you saw signs, but because you ate your fill of the loaves" (John 6:26). If we follow Christ for what we can get from him in the here and now, we are never going to feel full.

So how are we to think of Jesus? He told the crowd, "Do not labor for the food that perishes, but for the food that endures to eternal life, which the Son of Man will give to you." They did not understand what he was talking about, anymore than we do sometimes. They asked, "What must we do, to be doing the works of God?" Jesus answered, "This is the work of God, that you believe in him whom he has sent" (vv. 27–29).

Believing—it just seems too easy. There must be more to it than that. It is true that believing is simple, but it is not easy. It is actually one of the hardest things we will ever do. Believing in Jesus is true labor because, perverse as it sounds, we like things that are just a little more complicated. If all we have to do is believe, how can we feel that we are really accomplishing anything? How can we feel good about ourselves? We can't. Following Christ is to forgo the pursuit of getting full on ourselves or on the things we want in this life. This is true belief. We do not like it, and neither did the crowd listening to Jesus, which is why he added, "I am the bread of life; whoever comes to me shall not hunger, and whoever believes in me shall never thirst. But I said to you that you have seen me and yet do not believe" (vv. 35–36).

Believing is the simplest thing to do, and also the hardest, because it means we must let go of all attempts to believe in ourselves. But until we do that, we are going to feel hungry. If we allow Jesus to be our bread, our deepest hunger will cease for good. When we feed on Jesus, the bread of life, we will find that although we continue to desire the good things of this life, our longing for them no longer dominates our hearts.

> *One who is full loathes honey,*
> *but to one who is hungry everything bitter is sweet. (Prov. 27:7)*

Serving and Sitting

But Martha was distracted with much serving.

LUKE 10:40

*C*hristian burnout is a phrase we hear a good bit today, but it is nothing new. Christians have been burning out since the days of Martha. We are motivated to serve for all sorts of reasons. We certainly desire to serve our Lord, which is primary. We also serve to feel useful and to give purpose to our lives. And sometimes we serve simply because the Bible tells us to; we serve because it is the right thing to do.

Martha excelled at serving. And who wouldn't be motivated to serve like she did if Jesus came knocking at the front door? Her womanly heart yearned to take care of his creature comforts—a hot meal, a comfortable chair, perhaps some flowers on the table for visual appeal. Many of us open our homes in like manner to our guests. Others among us are quick to sign up to chair committees at church or to assist in the children's ministry. But sometimes in the midst of it all we find ourselves overwhelmed and frustrated—a natural response to adding too much to our already-busy lives or to serving for the wrong reasons.

If we find ourselves frustrated in our efforts to serve the Lord, perhaps God is trying to tell us something, which is exactly what happened with Martha. While racing around getting the meal on the table, making sure everything was just right, she spotted her sister Mary sitting on the floor just listening to Jesus. Martha was irritated at this and made her frustration known. "Lord, do you not care that my sister has left me to serve alone? Tell her then to help me," she complained (v. 40). But Jesus' response wasn't for Mary; his rebuke was for Martha: "Martha, Martha, you are anxious and troubled about many things, but one thing is necessary. Mary has chosen the good portion, which will not be taken away from her" (vv. 41–42).

It is clear that Jesus is much more concerned about our relationship with him than about what we do for him. He does not actually need us, but he knows how desperately we need him. That is why the Christian life is not serving. The Christian life is Christ. It is a relationship. Following Christ includes serving, but serving that leaves no room for the relationship becomes nothing more than self-serving, and it leads to frustration and burnout.

If we are burned out in our service for Christ, could it be that we have stopped sitting at Jesus' feet? Sometimes we serve because we are avoiding that quiet intimacy. For some reason, we don't want Jesus to get us alone. Maybe there is a sin we want to hang onto a little bit longer, or something that, while not overtly sinful, is pressing against our conscience nevertheless. It is often during such times that serving is actually easiest, because doing something for someone can be a slick way to bypass real intimacy. Even if we are unaware of a particular reason for avoiding Jesus, our fallen nature will invent all kinds of ways to keep us from getting too close. From all we know of Martha, that was not her reason for serving, but on that particular day she still missed out on what Mary gained.

Burnout is not an indicator that we need to try harder, work more, or reconfigure the calendar. It is an indicator that we need to stop what we are doing and get alone with God. Not later, when this project is done, when that retreat is over, or when the semester ends. If we want to enjoy the "good portion" that Mary enjoyed, we will do it now.

Life, Liberty, and the
Pursuit of Happiness

*Now there is great gain in godliness with contentment,
for we brought nothing into the world, and we
cannot take anything out of the world.
But if we have food and clothing, with these
we will be content.*

1 TIMOTHY 6:6-8

$\mathscr{H}$ere in 1 Timothy the Bible provides us with the formula to happiness, something we all want and something we seek. Our desire for happiness dictates our choices; it determines where we go and who we go there with. It determines what we do for a living and whom we marry. Our desire for happiness factors into why we read books like this. But we hesitate to admit it. Using the word *contentment* seems safer and much more within reach than outright happiness. Somehow *contentment* seems much more in keeping with godliness than *happiness*. But no matter which word we use, we are seeking one and the same thing. Let's not kid ourselves here—we know we are.

Our problem with the word *happiness* arises because we attach it to the things we acquire, whereas we link the word *contentment* to our hard-won ability to go without. But both of those definitions are wrong from a biblical standpoint; there, happiness and contentment are synonymous. In the Bible neither word is attached to the acquisition of things, nor do we find either word used to describe fortitude to go through the Christian life as a teeth-gritting ordeal. Godliness with contentment is great gain because godliness is holiness, which goes hand in hand with happiness. Reduced to its simplest equation, holiness equals happiness. Godliness, or holiness, is what we have been designed for, and if we are believers, it is our destiny. We are being conformed to Christ, who is himself perfect holiness. Therefore, the more like Christ we become, the holier we become, and we find ourselves increasingly happy.

In commenting about the Puritans, Elyse Fitzpatrick writes:

> What a shock it was to read of happiness from these men whom the world paints as grumpy, gloomy killjoys. For instance, Thomas Watson wrote, "[God] has no design upon us, but to make us happy"; and "Who should be cheerful, if not the people of God?" . . . The Puritans did not have in mind the shallow happiness experienced from temporal pleasures. They knew deep happiness was found in close relationship with God. It was available only to those who sought to be holy. "Those that look to be happy," Richard Sibbes wrote, "must first look to be holy." Notice that he didn't say, "Don't look to be happy," but rather, "Seek your happiness where it really is—in holiness."[1]

The "great gain" Paul is talking about here is the freeing realization that life does not consist of what we can get out of

[1]Elyse Fitzpatrick, *Idols of the Heart: Learning to Long for God Alone* (Phillipsburg, NJ: P&R, 2001), 84.

it. We came in with nothing, we will leave with nothing, and anything we get in between is fleeting and temporary. If we would just view our lives from this perspective, our capacity for joy would enlarge. Contentment would become much more than an occasional mood; it would characterize our entire life. The perspective Paul had in view here is an eternal one. He had a big-picture grasp of what life is all about, and because of that he realized that everything now is really for the purpose of what will happen later—a time that seems so far from us now but is really much closer than we realize. "Life is short," elderly people say, but they have lived long enough to know what they are talking about. "So teach us to number our days that we may get a heart of wisdom," prayed the psalmist (Ps. 90:12).

Holding that perspective is what enabled Paul to be utterly content with mere food and clothing, and it is why he said that the same happiness is available for all believers. Happiness, not the fleeting kind—the occasional good day—but the bound-out-of-bed-glad-to-be-alive kind, comes from running toward where God is ultimately taking us. The real source of all our unhappiness is due to the fact that we are running elsewhere. If we would just run in the right direction—toward Christ and his ways, toward the kingdom of God—we would find the happiness we are so desperately seeking, because that is the only place where it is to be found.

Whom have I in heaven but you?
    And there is nothing on earth that I desire besides you.
My flesh and my heart may fail,
    but God is the strength of my heart and my portion forever. (Ps. 73:25–26)